THE·STORY·OF·THE·CREATION·

·JANE·RAY·

ORCHARD BOOKS

For my mother and father

Copyright illustrations © Jane Ray 1992
First published in Great Britain in 1992 by
ORCHARD BOOKS
96 Leonard Street, London EC2A 4RH
Orchard Books Australia
14 Mars Road, Lane Cove, NSW 2066
1 85213 281 7
Printed in Belgium
The right of Jane Ray as illustrator of this work has
been asserted by her in accordance with the Copyright, Designs and Patents Act, 1988.
A CIP catalogue record for this book is available from the British Library.

This is how the world began.

In the beginning deep waters covered the earth, and it was empty and dark, without any shape. And God saw there was work for him to do.

God said, "Let there be light!" and there was light. And God divided the light from the darkness. He called the light day and the darkness he called night.

And the evening and the morning were the first day.

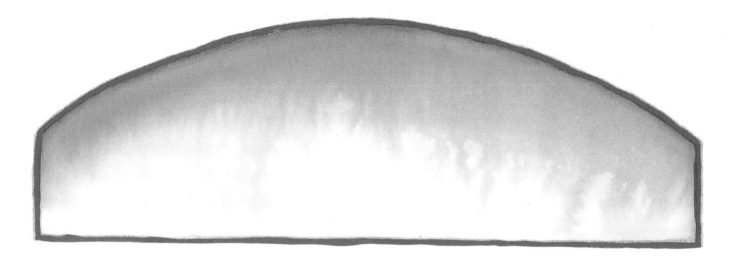

Then God divided the waters and made the arch of the sky.
And the evening and the morning were the second day.

On the third day, God gathered the waters into one place
and let the dry land appear.

God called the dry land earth and the waters he called the sea;
and he saw that it was good.

The waters rolled away and mountains and rocks and deserts and swamps appeared. And God said, "Let grass and trees and plants of every kind grow on the earth."

So the earth grew green and flowers bloomed and forests sprang up. The plants made seeds and spread themselves over all the earth.

And the evening and the morning were the third day.

January | February | March | April | May | June

Spring

Summer

On the fourth day God said, "Let there be lights in the sky to divide the day from the night, a great light called the sun to rule the day, and a lesser light called the moon to rule the night."

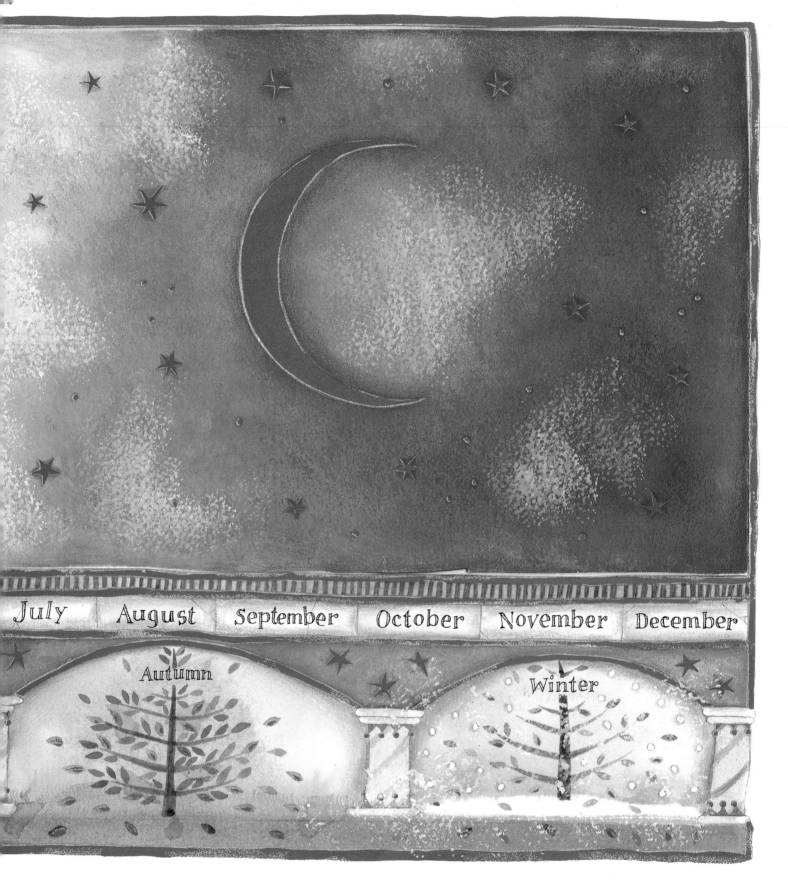

July   August   September   October   November   December

Autumn

Winter

God hung stars in the night sky. And as day followed night,
weeks, months, years and seasons could be counted.
And the evening and the morning were the fourth day.

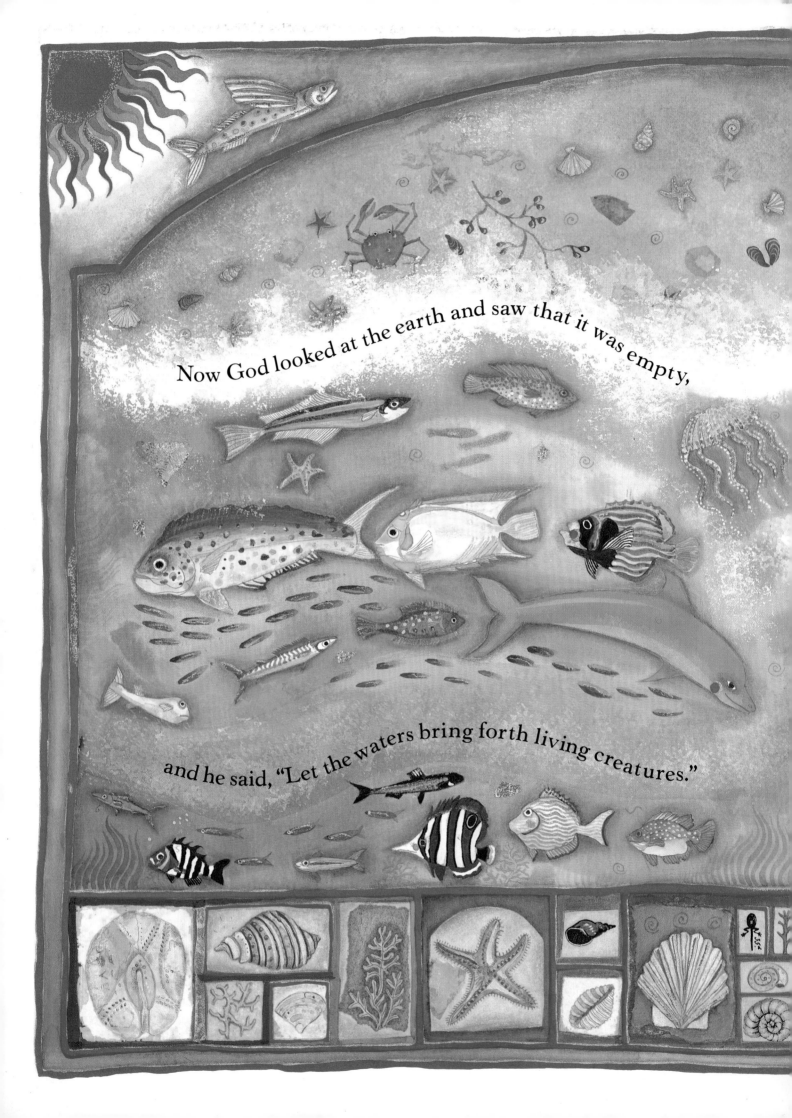

Now God looked at the earth and saw that it was empty, and he said, "Let the waters bring forth living creatures."

And he filled the seas with great whales and shoals of fishes, with dolphins, turtles, sharks, jellyfish, sealions, and sardines.

And the rivers and streams he filled with salmon and pike,
sticklebacks and minnows, otters, frogs and waterspiders.

Then God said, "Let there be birds on earth and to fly above the earth."

And the earth was filled with the song of birds as they rose into the sky:

peacocks and flamingoes, sunbirds and turtle doves, parrots,

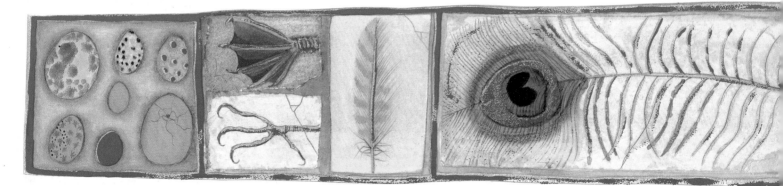

thrushes, owls, hummingbirds and nightjars.

And the evening and the morning were the fifth day.

On the sixth day God said,

"Let the earth bring forth every creature that moves,

cattle and creeping things, great beasts and small."

And every creature had its own place to live in, according to
its kind, and God saw that it was good.

But God had not finished his work.

He created man and woman in his own likeness, to take charge of the fish of the sea and the birds of the air and the beasts of the earth and everything that grows.

Adam and Eve gave a name to every creature they saw.

And God blessed Adam and Eve and all he had created and said, "Be fruitful and multiply and take care of the earth, so that it may last for ever."

And the evening and the morning were the sixth day.

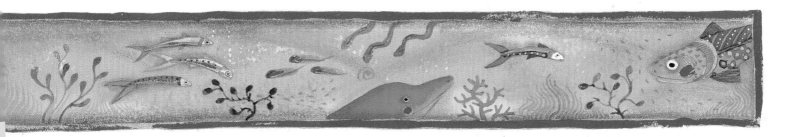

On the seventh day God finished his work, and he was pleased with what he saw. And God blessed the seventh day, and he rested.

And that is how the world began.